IN HIS
FOOTSTEPS

IN HIS FOOTSTEPS

Meditations on the Way of the Cross by
Father Ralph A. DiOrio

WITH NARRATIVE TEXT BY
Catherine Odell

PHOTOGRAPHS BY
Diane Garnette

IMAGE BOOKS
A Division of Doubleday & Company, Inc.
GARDEN CITY, NEW YORK
1986

Library of Congress Cataloging-in-Publication Data
DiOrio, Ralph A., 1930–
   In His footsteps.
      1. Jesus Christ—Crucifixion—Meditations.
2. Stations of the Cross. 3. Via Dolorosa (Jerusalem)
I. Odell, Catherine. II. Garnette, Diane. III. Title.
BT450.D57   1986   232.9′6   85-13180

ISBN: 0-385-19909-0

FOREWORD

Jesus gave to all Christians a route to righteousness, a road to the cross and Resurrection. It was the way that He Himself walked. During His entire life, He simply followed and accepted His Father's will. That in itself was not simple, but He knew that it was a loving will. And at the end, He made that will His own rationale for what otherwise would have been a senseless, agonizing Way of the Cross.

Because all Christians grow by following Jesus more faithfully, the actual Way of the Cross, the historic Via Dolorosa (Way of Sorrows) in Jerusalem, has always been deeply important to them. It has been the focus of fervent interest and endless research. It is the dearest parts of the Scripture remembered in time and space.

As early as the fourth century, the followers of Jesus wanted to go to the places where He had walked and talked and healed. But most of all, they wanted to go to the city where He died and rose from the dead. They wanted to walk the streets He walked on the road to victorious death.

An old but unsubstantiated tradition suggests that the Savior's mother had begun this custom, this return to the places Jesus graced with His presence. It is said that after his Ascension to heaven, she lovingly retraced the final steps of her son along the Via Dolorosa . . . a bittersweet pilgrimage.

Out of that Christian impulse to follow the mother's example grew the devotion called the Stations of the Cross. This custom most likely became common after the Crusades of the eleventh and twelfth centuries. The crusaders returned to Europe with their eyes aglow with the holy places and thoughts of the Passion of the Lord. In their own homes, many put together small tableaux to re-create the places where Jesus lived and died.

Gradually, the idea of small shrines or stations recalling the significant events of Christ's final hours became popular inside churches. Each station was to be a stopping point or station for meditation and prayer. The practice, in spirit at least, recapitulated pilgrimage.

In 1342, the Franciscans were given custody for the holy places in the Holy Lands. They promoted devotions to these sites and to the events which culminated in Good Friday's sacrifice. They began later to lead a procession along the Via Dolorosa at 3 P.M. every Friday afternoon, a custom that endures.

Through most of the Middle Ages, the number of these stations varied from place to place. In one town there were five stations or stops, while another town might show the pilgrim seven or eight stations. Even twenty or thirty stations were to be found.

In the eighteenth century, however, Pope Clement XII issued guidelines regularizing the practice. He also fixed the number of stops or stations at the modern number—fourteen. For all of the stations except one there is a historic and scriptural foundation. Scholars could find no real basis for the sixth station, the offering of the veil to Jesus by Veronica. But the followers of Jesus could find no better remembrance of Christ than to follow him all along the Way of the Cross.

A priest, an American, a man with a special calling to heal, has come to Jerusalem to do just this. He has never been to the Holy Land but to follow Jesus on His last walk has been a dream.

This priest will walk the Way of the Cross with the Lord he serves. It will be a painful journey as it always has been but it is, he is very sure, a necessary one. Thinking of the blessings God has given to his own ministry, this man in a white cassock shoulders his way slowly through the bustling Old City of Jerusalem on a Friday afternoon . . .

C.O.

INTRODUCTION

TO WALK WHERE JESUS WALKED

A spot dearly favored and often visited by Jesus was the quiet garden of Gethsemane, situated at the foot of the Mount of Olives. All those who visit the Holy Land today are urged by some power within their hearts to experience this important site. Its topography remains unchanged from the days of Jesus. In spite of the many newly erected cities spanning the Kidron Valley surrendering themselves to the progress of the ages, this little garden is still kept almost as it was at the time of Jesus. I received permission to spend two private hours of prayer there. It was a touching and unforgettable experience. Botanists believe that the roots of the original olive trees are still extant. In the silence and peacefulness of this secluded garden, Jesus found time, stillness, solitude and strength for renewed submission to His Father's will.

In my personal moments of praying there I could not help but relate the area to moments of Jesus. So often, no doubt, our Lord Jesus, after His own moments of personal intimate prayer with His dear Abba, His Father, must have risen from His knees and must have pensively gazed upward toward that gold-stoned city of Jerusalem. As He intently looked upon that "special city," He most certainly had often seen the smoke from the burning lambs being sacrificed by the priests in the Temple as they themselves were fulfilling their ritual duties. Jesus must have sighed with a divine and human sigh as His thoughts traversed its past, present and future scars. He must have whispered: O Jerusalem, you who burn animals in expiation, if you would only know, if you would only recognize, *I am the true Lamb to be sacrificed.*

Jerusalem did turn its back on Jesus. Jesus, on the other hand, and only by the Divine will, was to verify the Scriptures and the dramatic prophecies of old, e.g. (Isaiah 53:7), He was "like a lamb that is led to the slaughterhouse." *Jesus is the Lamb!* The Heavenly Father's purpose in sending His Son was to attest to the Father's commission in *the Lamb of God.* Jesus had come to die as a sacrificed lamb so that others in human flesh and in human bondage would be freed. He came to bring salvation to the unsaved; He came to refocus in wayward man God's Perspective, God's Purity, God's Power. He brought the *Good News.* He offered the *"new deal."* Through Him you and I have been given a new chance.

When that ugly moment came, the love of man dramatically and poisonously *turned sour.*

His love became *hate!* And hate *always finds a way to destroy.* Man's human hate gave Jesus a throne. They mounted that throne upon a garbage heap known as Calvary. It was a large rock rising approximately forty-five to fifty feet out of the ground. Its appearance resembled that of a skull. Today two chapels exist on that preserved platform. One, the site of the Crucifixion, is entrusted to the care of the Greek Orthodox. The other section—in two parts—belongs to the Roman Catholics and is believed to be the spots where Jesus was stripped of His garments and nailed to the cross. The actual rock of Calvary is visible through a grating under the altar dedicated to Mary, the Mother of Sorrows. This altar is called the thirteenth station. Here at these two altars I had the privilege of celebrating Holy Mass. It was truly a distinct opportunity for me to offer in an unbloody manner the very sacrifice of the mass which Jesus had offered on Good Friday in a bloody way. Upon that hill, too, I had spent moments of *intercessory redemptive prayer* at locations twelve and thirteen of the traditionally known devotions of the Way of the Cross. Station twelve is the actual point of crucifixion; station thirteen remembers the Lord Jesus being taken down from the throne of the cross and placed in the embracing arms of His Mother.

When Jesus was sentenced to die on Calvary's hill, his enemies—those who were perturbed, those who were prejudiced, the envious, the disquieted, the hypocritical, the apathetic, the religious and civic leaders of that period—cunningly manipulated the timeserving politicians and leaders. They used Pilate, the Roman governor, to sentence Jesus to the cross. In fact, anyone today who walks those particular areas of Jerusalem can almost hear again the shouting voices of the angry mob: "Crucify him! Crucify him! We have no king but Caesar!" Likewise, one can just about recapture the voice of Pilate, frightened over all this confusion, attempting at the same time to tone down his voice so as not to expose his human weakness, his fearful compromise, and thereby forfeit public respect. He steadies himself and feigns control when he utters, *"Ibis ad crucem!* You will go to the cross!"

And so the Master stumbled His way to Golgotha, by way of the cross—a painful way, step by step, fall by fall. His sacred feet touched those stones. His sacred divine and human blood dribbled upon those cobbled pathways, scarring them with crimson. The Way of the Cross is the steps Christ trod to Calvary. They serve as stepping-stones to redemption. Judea, with its harsh, bare hills, was not kind to its Savior Jesus as had been Galilee, with its gentle, enthusiastic crowds following Him. The Master's Galilean life had the happy aspect of an itinerant preacher and healer, a troubador of love proclaiming His gospel story. Judea, by contrast, represented the opportunity to save a sinful world.

In an attempt to be close to the Master along these traditionally recorded sites, the pilgrims find themselves pietistically involved and following the Way of Sorrows, also known as the Via Dolorosa, in Jerusalem. It was the way Jesus went to Calvary. The original roadway lies just below the present street. The pilgrim route is marked with fourteen stations, each point recalling some incident of that awful, excruciating journey. On Good Friday morning, and every Friday afternoon, Christian pilgrims march that route as Jesus did.

THE LOVE OF THE CRUCIFIED

Just as with human love the most tormenting thing is to be denied a love response from the person being loved, so it is with Christian love. The pilgrim's love response to Christ is sharing this arduous walk to Calvary. Following the Way of the Cross becomes a devotion of reciprocal love to the Suffering Savior. Love will always find a way for grateful expression.

This pilgrim walk, though, is merely commemorative. It honors the fourteen incidents of anguish and pain endured by our Lord Jesus as He staggered and stumbled from the place of condemnation, Pilate's palace, until His arrival on Calvary. Nine of these awful death-march incidents are creditably supported and fairly noted as *explicit* sites in the best historical accounts, namely those of the Holy Gospel. The other five have the authority only of implication or deduction. Other supportive sources derive from outpouring of devotion. When compared with the Gospel accounts, they would appear to be probable, although evidence is inconclusive.

Albert Storme in his booklet *The Way of the Cross** clarifies these questionable scenes as for their not being included in the Gospel narrative, but *as being certainly possible:*

> The Gospel accounts, when compared with the titles of the fourteen stations, are seen to omit the meeting of Jesus with his mother, the incident of the woman wiping the face of Christ, as well as the three falls. Each of these stations, however, appears to be very likely.
>
> Being present at the foot of the cross (John 19:25–27), Mary would have wished to see the procession pass by, with the apostle John and the women whose names we still know thanks to the Gospel (Mary, wife of Cleophas, Mary Magdalene, etc.). It is quite possible also that along the road were some of the noblewomen of the city,

---

* Kieran Dunlop, A.A., trans., *A Historical Sketch,* 2nd edition (revised), Franciscan Printing Press, Jerusalem.

who, in accordance with Jewish custom prepared soothing drinks for the condemned criminals. These charitable persons would be "Daughters of Jerusalem" whom Jesus exhorts not to lament over him, but rather over those responsible for his death. The narrow crowded streets would have facilitated the brave, generous gesture of one of these women who, cloth in hand, approached the Prisoner to wipe his face. Legend has given her the immortal name of Veronica.

As for the falls, regardless of their number, they are understandable in a man exhausted and subjected to great moral and physical suffering from the day before. They explain the commandeering of a certain Simon, native of the northern coast of Africa.

Tremendous spiritual benefit is derived by the faithful who meditate over these scenes even though history and legend are mixed, even though the nonevangelical scenes remain in question. For the most part they are valued by commentators who see them as simple suppositions or even as pure legends.

The historical, violent human deed of murdering Jesus traditionally links those major events involved with the carrying of the cross through some of those alleys and streets. For the sensitive Christian heart, the awful death walk commemorates the last precious moments and episodes of the Passion. It moves the pilgrim to venerate and pray.

Because it is so natural for pilgrims, both of the past and of the present, to want to respond with their love in gratitude to the Suffering One, there arose in the West a desire to accompany our Lord Jesus not only in spirit but also in a physical way, along the road to Golgotha.

The Way of the Cross is an opportunity for personal reflection and soul communication with our God. It was God Who determined *the Good Effect:* that is, mankind's opportunity for insight into his relationship with his God, his chance for a new birth experience through contrition, the incredible gift of God for *reconciliation, redemption, regeneration,* and *righteousness.* Come, now, and walk that ancient Way. Come just as you are. Follow Jesus. The Lord does not question that you are not worthy or ask why you have erred. All that He asks is, Why don't you come back to Me?

PREPARE MY HEART, O LORD

These sorrowful stations become mankind's prayer points, physical contacts, means to communicate with heaven. Through these stations of meditation and prayer all peoples from every land and nation are able to elevate their immortal souls toward their God—*to adore*

Him, to praise Him, and to thank Him. St. Augustine in his discourse on the Psalms (Psalms 148:1–2; CCL, 40, 2165–2166) states:

> Our thoughts in this present life should turn on the praise of God, because it is in praising God that we shall rejoice forever in the life to come; and no one can be ready for the next life unless he trains himself for it now. So we praise God during our earthly life, and at the same time we make our petitions to Him.

Let us now pray:

Lord, I worship You and I praise You. Because of Your cross You redeemed me, You redeemed the whole world. I want to be Your devotee in the true sense of the word. Thrust me, dear Lord, right into myself that I may come out of myself a new Christlike person responding to that piety in the compassion of following You on the sorrowful way of the Passion. Accept me, Lord, as a companion of consolation. May my human love respond to You Who are Love.

R.A.D.

JESUS IS CONDEMNED
TO DEATH

It is a chilly March or April morning shortly before Passover in the year we now call A.D. 30. In a Roman courtyard in Jerusalem's Fortress Antonia, a blood-drenched, breathless man awaits the words which will send Him to His death. He is in agonizing pain. He has just received a brutal whipping from ruthless Roman guards who spell one another with a metal-tipped scourge. With hands bound, with no friends to defend Him, He stands—an innocent man about to be sent to His death in the prime of life. He stands as the Son of God prepared to die for mankind. His name is Jesus Christ.

It is a summer day almost two thousand years later in a year we now call our own day. In the courtyard of El Omariyeh College, a Roman Catholic priest with a mighty ministry of healing stands remembering that Man of Sorrows who also stood here. On this spot, the Fortress Antonia long ago towered above the city streets of the Jewish Holy City. With a growing and clearly God-given mission in the United States, he has come to the Holy Land to walk in the footsteps of the Divine Healer. He has come on pilgrimage to see, feel, taste and hear the message Jesus left along the Via Dolorosa, the Way of the Cross. His name is Ralph Anthony DiOrio.

In the city of Jerusalem, the city where Jesus suffered, died and rose from the dead, the present and the past are often hard to separate. Far below the surface of the landscaped little courtyard where Father DiOrio now stands with his head in a New Testament are the foundations of the old Antonia.

Probably, the sky is quite a different hue from what it was on the morning Jesus stood here. In the El Omariyeh courtyard where Father DiOrio lingers, other things are also clearly different. A large, proud palm rises from the small landscaped square in the middle of the court. A sampling of the Holy Land's wild flowers circles the palm as if to say that there is reason for joy as well as grief here.

The building and court, of course, are much younger structures than the ones that bring pilgrims here. Most of the college building was rebuilt in 1838, but inside is preserved a small but beautiful chapel called the Chapel of the Crowning of Thorns.

But there is something more than the undeniable remains of old buildings resting below new buildings here. Something in the earth and air seems to say that God who was here in a special way is present still. For Father DiOrio, it must seem as though the events of two thousand years ago are not really over. And in a sense, they aren't. On this ground, Jesus Christ was once condemned to die. Above the grave of the Antonia, even the stones remember . . .

It was here in midmorning that Jesus stood flanked by two Roman guards. King Herod had built this fort to protect the northeast quarter of Jerusalem. In A.D. 6, it had come into Roman hands. Over a thousand soldiers were stationed here now very near the Temple grounds. Pontius Pilate, the procurator of the southern provinces, had arrived from Caesarea soon after dawn. He sat under a Mediterranean blue sky listening to "one more complaint of the Jews."

Pilate's seat was raised on a platform above the flagstone square used for public audiences or trials. His seat the Romans called a *bema*. Roman justice was handed down from the bema in the open air here in Jerusalem. The stone courtyard where crowds of angry Jews were now assembling was known as the Lithostratos (a Greek word meaning "paved") courtyard. But Pilate wasn't happy at the decree these Jews were asking of him.

His aides had just told the procurator that the High Priest Caiaphas and others were asking the death sentence for the Galilean teacher named Jesus since he had already been "convicted" of blasphemy. He claimed to be the "Son of the Holy One," they said, and that

offense cried out for execution according to
their own Book of Numbers.

But it was easy to see that the Jewish leadership was jealous of Jesus. Now they were
claiming he was guilty as well of civil crimes:
sedition and claiming to be "king." They were
raising those charges because Pilate could not
condemn Jesus for a religious offense. Since the
Jews were forbidden to execute, they depended
upon Pilate. The situation was starting up a
headache in the temples of the procurator. He
resented the whole lot of them.

Pilate, his face angled toward the morning
sun, suddenly looked at the Prisoner. This was
no insurrectionist! He had just had this Jesus
scourged, a usual prelude to crucifixion. He
could barely stand. Thirty minutes earlier, Pilate had questioned Him inside his own Antonia quarters. The other Jews would not go in
the dwelling of a non-Jew on the eve of Passover for fear of defilement. They didn't need to
worry. Jesus of Nazareth said nothing in His
own defense. But this Galilean . . . His eyes
had searched Pilate's and touched him deeply.
There was no hatred, only love.

Now, however, the walls of the Antonia
were ringing with cries for the Prisoner's
blood. Suddenly, Pilate was afraid of this mob.
A riot would stain his record. The shadow cast
by the Antonia's massive tower lay across the
Lithostratos. With a chill moving down his
back, the procurator saw that it pointed to the

bloody feet of Jesus. He could do no more. He reached for the quill and signed his name to the order. "Crucifixion!" he shouted to a cheering crowd.

Meditation

SENTENCED

Lord Jesus, I stand before You with all the brokenness of my personal weaknesses. You are standing with all the perfection of Your human and divine strength: You stand before a portion of the world's cruelty, an irrational mob. They are infuriated. Their own inadequacies prompt their unrest, which they project upon You. Such is the evil of displaced anxiety. You are their scapegoat!

Pilate publicly states: *"Ecce homo!"* But this stiff-necked mob *won't listen!* They are like little children, determined on their own wishes. They place their fingers in their ears. They poison Pilate into fear. He surrenders in cowardly fashion, becoming their channel of hatred, and *they give You sentence.* What a climax of human malice! But in contrast, You offer what *only a God* can offer: *the climax of Divine Love.*

As I meditate upon this first station, what precisely does my prayer express? Let me enter more profoundly into my prayer. Let me have God's Perspective. There is the tumultuous clamor of the enemies of God, of Jesus and of His sanctifying Holy Spirit. It was so tumultuous that its evil spirit prevailed over the timeserving politician Pontius Pilate. It disclosed him as weak and frightened, a coward like all enemies. And so Pilate, the governor, became the governed. The mob conquered him.

The historical fact remains: Pilate yielded to their evil spirit's murderous demands. He, a mere human, passed sentence upon Jesus, the Divine. He delivered Jesus up to the soldiers. They would prepare Jesus for Calvary. They would crucify Him. And to fulfill that death sentence, Pilate and his officials cast upon Jesus a cross.

Though there is no trace of a judicial sentence of condemnation recorded in the proceedings of the criminal Christ, there nevertheless remains the fact that Pilate said: "I am innocent of this man's blood. It is your concern" (Matthew 27:24).

What a flagrant *injustice!* This heathen governor, Pilate, made a feeble attempt, against his very own conscience, mind you, to bring about Jesus' liberation. And even though he had at his disposal a military garrison, he nevertheless became a *victim of compromise.* He actually enslaved himself, as many humans do at times. And so he turned his back on God: he betrayed truth. He walked away from Jesus.

And to hide from the immorality of his conduct, he played the part dramatically well. He called for the basin to wash his hands of everything. He allowed the servant to pour slowly the vessel's contents. But as that water dropped and sprinkled itself, appearing like glittering jewels in the early morning sun, he gruffly pronounced to Jesus: *"Ibis ad crucem!* You will go to the cross!"

My Lord, help me never again to compromise You. Help me never again to sin against You. Please, Lord, teach me how to serve You with all my heart: to know what it really means to love, to adore. Help me, Lord. All I can offer at this moment are my tears of repentance with heart and eyes open that I may see You, my God!

JESUS RECEIVES HIS CROSS

Out of the court of El Omariyeh College, Father Ralph DiOrio walks to follow the painful path of Jesus. The journey takes the pilgrim down the street to turn into El Wad Street. The way of the Via Dolorosa is narrow and steep as it has always been. Hugging the stone-faced streets constructed a century after Christ are the small shops where everything from housewares to meats to olive-wood souvenirs to rock records is sold today. Even in the days of Jesus, this quarter was filled with merchants. Today, in the square kilometer of space which the Old City occupies, more than one thousand shops vie for the attention of the pilgrims of many faiths.

But before Jesus entered the street from the Antonia, Roman soldiers hauled him to one corner of the courtyard from the middle. On his shoulders, they laid the crossbar or crossbeam of the cross. The upright onto which it would soon be hoisted was already in place at Golgotha, the place of crucifixion. Before it was hoisted up, the outstretched arms of Jesus would be nailed to it at the wrists.

Today, authorities suggest that this sort of

crossbeam may have weighed about a hundred pounds. Laying the heavy wood beam across His lacerated shoulders and back added to the mounting agonies of Christ. Then, the Prisoner was led through the busiest sections of the city. Forcing the condemned to carry the instrument of his own destruction added to the ignominy of the sentence. This display was to act as a deterrent to others, the Romans reasoned. And surely, they should have been right.

Crucifixion, ancient writers attested, was a horrid death. The victim's pain was second only to that suffered by those burned alive, but the torture of crucifixion was longer. The crucified might live for days, succumbing finally to dehydration or asphyxiation. Yet this was the form of capital punishment then commonly used by Rome in her conquered provinces. It was not used on Roman citizens. Later, in the fourth century, the Christian emperor Constantine ended its use altogether in remembrance of the Savior Who died on a cross.

Father DiOrio quietly comes to the place that serves as the second station of the cross. It is simplicity itself. There is only a marker in the high white stone wall. This station marks the reality of Christ's first steps toward death with His cross. But here on the street, pedestrians detour around the priest contemplating the sad beginning of such a journey.

Opposite the station marker, there is the

Chapel of the Condemnation, which stands on the Lithostratos. In fact, each of the stations was complemented with a small chapel along the Via Dolorosa. This chapel and several others are small but necessary retreats. The streets are often noisy and filled with the sort of free-wheeling city commotion that makes pilgrims think twice about stopping long to pray.

But for a moment Father DiOrio has the narrow passageway of Jesus to himself. His Scripture falls open where the Passion of Jesus is already marked. The words of the evangelist Mark are short but sharp. "They led him out to crucify him" (Mark 15:21).

Did He stumble to this side of the street beneath the cross? What was He thinking when some were weeping for Him and others were jeering at Him? Were any of His frightened friends or apostles hidden and watching in the crowd?

The answers, of course, will never be known. What is known is that Jesus Christ suffered with every step, with every breath He took along His Way of the Cross.

Meditation

CONDEMNED TO A CROSS

The road to Calvary begins. The road to Golgotha is the climax of human malice. It is like human love gone sour from hatred. The beautiful paradox is that Love—with its extinguishing and quenching power of a *loving holy spirit* —overrides the power of human hatred.

The bloody road to Calvary where Jesus walked and stumbled enters the pages of human history as nothing more than *mankind's intrusion into the original created plan of the Almighty.* But in God's perspective of Divine Providence, that human intrusion remains *God's invitation to participate in redeeming salvation.* By condemning Jesus to the cross, man in his confused anger allowed his hatred to tap the infinite love of the Divine. Man's hatred toward Christ through Calvary really permitted the Almighty to love him through His Christ on Calvary. Such are the paradoxes of love both with man and with God. Calvary was evil men's way and purpose to put an end to *this disturbing Christ;* but God's purpose was to redeem the hateful accusers through the love of the Redeemer. God made the road to Calvary a stepping way to heaven.

And so Jesus received the condemnation of crucifixion; He accepted it for the glory of His Father, and for His ordained mission: salvation for those who would receive it.

Lord Jesus, the hatred of man, dwelling persistently in sin, thrust upon Your human divine shoulders a universe of crosses. As soon as Pilate had approved the unjust sentence of death for You, those barbarous soldiers—gruff and monstrously cruel—seized You as hungry dogs would seize their prey. They violently pushed You forth to the beam of the tree.

> . . . and carrying his own cross he went out of the city to the place of the skull or, as it was called in Hebrew, Golgotha. (John 19:17)

What a painful and rough journey awaited You, dear Jesus! Have mercy on us, dear Lord. In Your kindness, in Your compassion, blot out our offenses.

Station Three

JESUS FALLS THE FIRST TIME

Very close to the second station, pilgrims turn the corner into El Wad Street for the third stopping place or station of the cross. Tradition, rather than Scripture, suggests that Jesus fell to the ground here beneath His cross. And yet the Gospels of Matthew, Mark and Luke do substantiate that the Savior was too weak to bear His cross by Himself to the end of the Via Dolorosa.

At this third marker, Father DiOrio looks up at the stone relief of an exhausted Jesus fallen beneath a full cross. The work is finely done and is set beneath an arch over a door which leads to the station chapel. To the left of the doorway and the station, a waist-high portion of a stone column helps to support the iron railing in front of the station.

Until 1947, this column, lying broken upon the ground, marked this station remembering the fallen, broken Jesus. The Polish Army, stationed in Palestine until Israeli independence, restored the chapel, erected the stone relief below the arch and realized the proper place that the "fallen" column should have here. It is a moving, quiet statement in stone.

If Jesus did fall here on the Via Dolorosa, it would have been tragically predictable aside from the weight of the crossbar He carried.

Scourging, that savage preparation for crucifixion, was in fact a Roman gesture of compassion. It so weakened the victim with injuries and loss of blood that the death agony on the cross would be shortened. But this weakening of Jesus also prepared the way for His collapse to the Lithostratos beneath the cross. If He was unable to break His fall, the wood beam undoubtedly pounded down on top of His back and His head, already tortured with a crown of long-thorned acanthus.

It is also clear that Jesus would probably have been light-headed and fatigued at this point, even without the physical punishment. The night before had been a sleepless one. And it is very likely that He had been given nothing to eat after His arrest. The Gospels report that when Pilate issued the decree of condemnation, it was close to the sixth hour of the day (noon). Jesus had probably been without food for more than fifteen hours—since the Passover meal He had shared with His apostles the evening before.

And stress—what about the effects of stress on Jesus?

Only in modern times have medical authorities begun to calibrate the cost of stressful situations on the human body. It is now known that stress is a major contributor to the six

leading causes of death in the United States.
And even in the short run, unrelieved tensions
or emotional traumas can result in stomach
distress, headache, muscular cramping, a rise
in blood pressure and other disorders.

No Gospel account can fully capture the
emotional and psychological suffering which
befell the Son of God in His last days. It is
clear that He had known perfectly well what
His fate would be for some time before His
death. Upon that understandable anxiety was
then layered the additional abuses of His last
day of life.

Not one of His closest friends stood with
Jesus when His need for emotional support
and love would have been greatest. The taunt-
ing and humiliation inflicted by the Roman
soldiers and the personal guards of Herod
Agrippa, the king of Galilee, were vicious and
unchecked. Under Roman law, there was no
limit on what modern law would label "cruel
and unusual punishment." In fact, there was
no relief at all for Jesus during His last misera-
ble hours.

As Father DiOrio turns to continue up El
Wad Street, the words of the Psalmist come to
mind. Surely they also echoed in the heart of
Jesus of Nazareth as He stumbled up this
street.

> Yahweh my God, I call for help all day,
> I weep to you all night;

may my prayer reach you
hear my cries for help;

for my soul is all troubled,
my life is on the brink of Sheol;
I am numbered among those who go down
to the Pit,
a man bereft of strength . . .

(Psalms 88:1–4)

FALL NUMBER 1

Without some kind of faith there can be no hope. What would we be if we were left both to our own unreliable resources and to the irrational brutalities of human anger displayed through human cruelty? David once said that he would prefer to be judged by God rather than by men.

O Jesus, You fell beneath the cross! That fall had to happen. With such a load upon Your shoulders it just had to be expected. Your human nature tried desperately to be brave, to wax strong under the weight of that heavy wooden tree. Only Your persistent love for us did not allow evil where evil erupted. What evil men would attempt to destroy by hate You persistently attempted to transform through love. You would support, sustain, us ignorant and fickle creatures. Like a lamb led to slaughter, befogged, baffled, stunned at the objective reality of man's turning love into hate, You went forward in silence. In silence, You bore those human outrages. Your attitude is tremendously different from *my own retaliative reactions* to acts of human cruelty and irrational or passionate behavior. So often we humans claim righteousness when we too are secretly guilty. So often we respond with *rebellion* and *revenge*. Lord, I can take responsibility only for myself, not for another's conscience. I can only lament my own misfortune and wonder why I am thought ill of.

Lord, as I observe You trying to march courageously to Calvary, bearing the crossbeam upon Your shoulders, my mind reflects how, according to ancient tradition in the believing body of the Church, this devotional station of the cross confirms that You must have fallen to the ground not just once, nor twice, but many times. After all, is it not understandable that a man exhausted as You were and subjected as You were to such ignominious moral and physical torments from the evening before would certainly fall?

Regardless of the number of the falls, the Christian lover contemplates Your falling at least three times under the heavy weight of the Cross. That death march was a rugged experience. No food, no drink, had entered You since the Last Supper. The tormenting, excruciating lashings drained much blood. The various types of inflictions heaped upon You at the whim of the soldiers weakened You, fatigued You so!

The cross, too, was definitely a crude, unshaven beam of heavy wood. Its burden essentially compressed within itself *my sins*. So often I have repeated my same weaknesses. So often, immediately after making fresh resolves, I allowed persons and things to preoccupy my life again with their false promises. I am sorry for the consequences. I must still pay for my weakness, even though You have forgiven me. Nature is on God's side; and it will be remedied.

Dear Lord, by Your endurance, by Your unchangeable love, help me to repent my human falls. By the strength of Your passion and suffering, I will try to arouse from within me the human person You meant me to be—a person according to Your Own Heart!

Station Four

JESUS MEETS HIS MOTHER

Like the third, the fourth station of the cross is the work of the Polish artist T. Zieliensky. In a beautiful stone relief presentation above the door to a small station oratory or chapel, the continuing tragedy of the journey of Jesus is presented. Here, the aching, bleeding, tortured Son meets his grief-stricken mother. The horror of it all is reflected in her face as she reaches to touch the hand of Jesus supporting His cross.

It is a moving portrait and Father DiOrio stands beneath it and the sun for some moments. The enormous pain that Mary, the mother of Jesus, must have known at this moment! Again, the subject of the station is conjectural rather than scriptural. Only the evangelist John speaks of Mary's presence during the Passion and death of Jesus. That was the scene at the cross where Jesus was already crucified and close to death.

Nonetheless, the tradition that mother and Son met along the Way of the Cross is a very old one and there is some reason to believe that it might be historical.

Not far from the fourth station stands the

Armenian church Our Lady of the Spasm.
This church is little more than a century old.
Like so many places in the Old City, however,
its foundation rests on the rubble of antiquity.
Once, a church named St. Sophia rose above
this place.

When Our Lady of the Spasm Church was
being built, excavations unearthed an elabo-
rately framed mosaic depicting two feet point-
ing to the northwest. This was the direction
from which Jesus came down the stone-paved
street carrying His cross. The mosaic was
judged to be more than one thousand years old
and had most likely been displayed in St. Sophia. It is likely that it was an object of prayerful veneration. The mosaic represented Mary's
feet and the place where she stood when she
met her Son.

What did Jesus say to her? Did Mary have
any time to put her own feelings into words?
Or did the Romans shove the Condemned
along before any sense of sympathy could stir
the crowd?

In the culture of this mother and Son, such a
moment of last farewells was even more devas-
tating. Jesus was the only Son of his widowed
mother in a society in which a woman was almost totally dependent upon a father or hus-
band or son. Mary would soon be without any
of these, the most reliable means of support.
But Jesus, the Final Healer, remedies this tragedy from His cross, as John reports. Mary is

given another son, John, by her dying Son Jesus. John is given Mary as mother.

It is hard for pilgrims to move on from this station of sad encounter and Father DiOrio feels the pull of it. The thought of mother and Son sharing each other's special agony in the midst of an excited, shoving crowd is transfixing.

A MOTHER MEETS THE SON

History is filled with the devotion of mothers toward their children. A great mother is the finest legacy a child can have. Mothers live and die with their children. So often, and very silently, a mother suffers with them and for them. Untold sacrifices will never be known—how often a mother cared for her children and bore with them their every anguish. She lives with them and too often dies with them. Mothers who must live on after their children's death, if that be the destiny, survive on last looks.

The fourth station of the Way of the Cross speaks of such survival. Mary, whom God the Father had chosen from all eternity to be the mother of His Son, the Christ, knew that her Son Jesus was destined to save mankind. She also so well knew without a shadow of a doubt that the Almighty had loved her and had chosen her to be the physical channel for the mystery of the Incarnation. Through her God became flesh; God became man that man might become God. What a Mystery of Divine Redemption! She accedes to God's will—for that is all she ever tried to do. And as she humbly did, she heard the angel say His name, Emmanuel!

Life is not always filled with joys and pleasures. The happy days of Bethlehem and of Nazareth hastily passed. And now a very tragic moment had arrived. Simeon's prophecy, as recorded by St. Luke (2:33–35), had come to fruition. It was the exact moment of a mother's deepest sorrow. Scripture definitely gives her an historical place, one which will never be taken from her, at *the foot of the cross.* St. John was next to her and later wrote: "Near the cross of Jesus stood His mother . . ." (John 19:25–27).

The crib was not the only place where she was to be remembered (see Luke 2:7: ". . . she gave birth to a son, her first-born. She wrapped him in swaddling clothes"); but it gave her perennial implicit honor, as without question or doubt this holy mother who was at Calvary beneath the cross *had to have trodden* the same pathway as her condemned Son. She was a mother; and that was her place! She had to have walked and have run with rapid pace. And as she attempted to get near to her son, she could only follow those sacred blood spots shed by Him.

As Jesus moved on His way to Golgotha, jostled along by the rude and crude and boisterous officials, who ill treated Him, urged Him to quicken His steps, He suddenly had to endure another immense pain. There before

His bloodshot eyes was His dear mother. There she was on the very path He was treading. O my God! What a meeting! Disgrace! Dishonor! Flesh and blood appearing so cheap! Between the two holy ones, Jesus and Mary, Son and mother, there was trembling grief, eyes meeting in expressions of understanding for the other's soul, spiritual penetrations into the mysterious ways of Divine Providence. And all that they had to sustain them was *love*.

Dear Mary, dear mother of Jesus, my spiritual mother, your presence at the passion of Jesus causes me to want all the more a deeper comprehension of the gravity, the seriousness, of human sins. All sin is evil. It cannot go hand in hand with God. It is either one or the other. Human sins, including mine, gave pain and death to the body of your Son Jesus. In offending Jesus, your Son, those very same sins offend and embarrass you. All sin is blushingly embarrassing.

Dear Mary, mother of Jesus, my spiritual mother, take me as Jesus consigned me to you and you to me. Be my mother! Take me as I am, a sinner. Pray for me now and at the hour of my death. And at my death, take me by the hand as only a mother can and bring me safely to the feet of Jesus, Who will present me to the Father.

SIMON HELPS JESUS TO CARRY HIS CROSS

Leaving the place where Jesus is said to have left His mother, Father DiOrio threads through a growing crowd to the corner. He smiles thank-yous and returns hellos to the Arab shopkeepers seated on their stools outside places where stores with religious goods, camera film, olive-wood artwork, clamor for tourist attention one on top of another. One shop boldly names itself after the station of the cross which faces it across the stone street.

It is here that the Way of the Cross seems to increasingly wind through a commercial zone. It's a shocking reality to some Christians but a state of affairs not so different from the setting that Jesus encountered along the same walk.

"Come in, please," a young Arab calls, getting up from his wooden stool. He gestures toward the bank of olive-wood statues displayed on a card table right outside the shop. Something in this priest's face seems to strike this businessman as receptive. Smiling wooden shepherd boys mingle with three-piece settings of the Holy Family and foot-high renditions of camels. Samplings of sacred and secular sub-

jects offer something for everyone. "Hey, Father, we have many good buys . . . and for
you, an even better price."

But Father DiOrio's "Maybe later" seems
resolute. The young man sits down again beneath the Jerusalem noonday sun shining
straight overhead. It is a pleasant but busy
hour in this Moslem quarter of the city
through which the Way of the Cross must pro-
ceed.

Father DiOrio reaches the corner of the
street. A backward look over the shoulder at
this point makes one think of an alley through
a gold- or buff-bricked canyon. But it is a narrow canyon. From the door of a shop on one
side of the street to the stone or brick wall on
the other side is no more than a dozen feet.

Yet the Via Dolorosa is not completed and
the priest who is here to follow it turns the
corner to the right and continues up the street.
This street is actually named the Street of Dolors, or Tareem el Alam. The climb becomes
quite steep and gives reason for the placement
of the fifth station just to the left around the
corner.

By the time Jesus reached this place, most of
the distance from the Antonia to Golgotha had
already been covered. From the beginning to
the end, the Way of the Cross would have been
no more than four hundred to five hundred
yards, or roughly a quarter of a mile. For
Jesus, however, even the short distance re-

maining was now too much. As the route begins to climb at a fairly steep angle, Jesus could no longer manage it with the cross across His shoulders. The Roman centurion overseeing the execution had a decision to make.

As his title implies, one hundred soldiers were under the command of this Roman. Most probably, the full contingent had been assigned to control the crowds and force a path for the condemned (Jesus and the other two), all the way to Calvary. But the crowds were growing larger in this midday rush. Passover errands and all business had to cease completely by sundown, about 6 P.M.

A man named Simon, the Synoptic Gospels report, was entering the city just at this moment. It is clear that he was entering through a gate that no longer exists, possibly coming in from work in the fields to the northwest.

Simon was a native of Cyrene, a city of northern Africa. At least in the centurion's eyes, this was a Jew he could force into service for Jesus and for the sake of Roman justice. So Simon, who was probably a farmer, was ordered to shoulder the heavy wooden beam. Then he fell in line behind a weakening, exhausted Jesus and the four Romans assigned to the Nazarene's execution detail.

To have commanded the same service of a nearby Jew of prominence could have started a riot. Carrying the crossbeam was part of the sentence handed down. But the centurion was becoming afraid that Jesus would die before He reached the execution site. The sentence of Pilate would then be thwarted and the procurator might become angry.

Who was this Simon who steps into the Gospel accounts out of nowhere?

There is no indication that this Simon was at this point a follower of Jesus. The evangelist Mark identifies him, however, as the father of Alexander and Rufus, two disciples later well known to the Christian community in Rome. Simon, a man with the same name as the absent friend of Jesus, merely appears at the right moment. Then his steps follow the Master's along the Via Dolorosa. He takes up a burden he hasn't chosen.

A plaque mounted above a heavy wooden door marks the place where this incident is called to mind. The plaque is inscribed in Latin. The dark wood door admits pilgrims to the fifth station oratory. This small chapel for prayer was erected by the Franciscans in the last century. In fact, the site had been in their hands in the thirteenth century soon after the Crusades. On this spot, the custodians of the holy places had made their first Holy Land home.

Unlike the third and fourth stations, this is a very simple memento of the cross that was taken up by Simon here. There is only the inscription. Possibly, however, its simplicity enables every Christian who walks this way to see here the burden of the cross being transferred to his own shoulders. Simon, after all, can be seen as a symbol of every follower of Jesus.

"If anyone wants to be a follower of mine, let him renounce himself and take up his cross and follow me," Jesus had warned his followers long before He saw His own Calvary cross (Mark 8:35). Father DiOrio closes his Testament, lingers for a moment there and then joins the crowd moving up the street.

A STRANGER BECOMES
A FRIEND

Jesus, you needed a *helper on the way.*

Jesus stumbled, to and fro. The splintery cross was becoming exceptionally heavy. The coarse tree beam of freshly chopped wood was irritating the wounds already inflicted upon Jesus' holy flesh. His innocence caused His pain to become all the more intense. The splinters hurt deeply; and each splinter was of a different size; some were small, some large. Some even fell into His opened fresh wounds. The pain was exhausting, horrible! His skin was bleeding, and blood poured copiously from His wounds. His flesh erupted into bubbling holes. Oh *how it hurt!*

The patrol officer looked at his prisoner. The patrol officer, centurion as he was called, definitely did not want Jesus to die on the roadway. This Nazarene had to be crucified, and that was it! But the centurion, realizing the exhaustion, weakness and near-depletion of his Prisoner, while intending to torture the Prisoner most completely on Calvary with the torment of crucifixion by nails, now looked about the crowd. There before him came the solution to the dilemma. He forcefully hustled a by-stander who in a moment of curiosity stopped to see what the awful parade was about. The centurion commandeered the man into service. The man's name was Simon. He was a black man, a native of the northern coast of Africa.

And so it came to be that Simon of Cyrene, an African, is *the chosen one* called to carry the cross for redemption. With Jesus he walked, first as a resentful, frightened stranger. He had never before experienced such humiliation. But suddenly, looking for one brief moment into the eyes of the unfortunate wretch condemned to death, Simon not only perceived with human organs of sight, he envisioned Jesus' divine holy spirit. That spirit penetrated him with warmth. He experienced a fiery baptism of love. There was no longer any room for resentment, anger or humiliation. Strength entered his own soul. He smiled at Jesus and with a breath of freedom began to walk the load upon his black shoulders. In that moment of grace, the stranger became a friend to the Divine. And so together, God and the African carried the burden of human slavery up the hill of purifying and redemptive love.

St. Matthew's Gospel (27:32) records: "On their way out, they came across a man from Cyrene, Simon by name, and enlisted him to carry his cross." Just as it is divine love that is calling certain disciples, so it was a mysterious dispensation of Divine Providence which summoned this black man, Simon, *to share the carrying of the cross.* What a beautiful introduction by Jesus of Himself to this stranger who would by God's Holy Spirit become a regenerated righteous devotee of this crucified Master! What Jesus was really doing to that helper was offering him a baptism of fire. If he, like the apostles chosen by Jesus to be His living ambassadors, could experience the presence of Jesus, His passion and His death, then Simon of Cyrene *would* continue the story of the Crucified One throughout the passage of his own years. He would be an authentic witness!

Speaking quite literally, and also in harmony with the concept of *water and the Spirit,* what Jesus did to Simon was baptize him with the Holy Spirit and with fire! Morally frightened over that incident, though physically robust, this poor African was simply like many of us: only a vessel of clay. Like all of us who are called by Jesus to bear the burden of the apostolic mission of redemption, Simon received in that moment of grace a real cleansing and then the hardening by spiritual fire because God is a Consuming Fire! The Holy Spirit is needed to make us perfect and to renew us, because only spiritual fire can cleanse, and only spiritual water can recast each of us, making us into new men and women, pleasing and favorable to God.

Lord Jesus, everything in Your life from Your birth to Your Passion and death as Redeemer and Risen Savior is holy; it is sacred! Lord, You have a simple unpretentious way, so characteristic about You, of knowing how to fill everyone, if we only let You, with distinctive grace for special living. You are filled with such mystery! This incident with Simon of Cyrene from the North African coast was no mere accident. To some it may appear trivial. But it has significance; it illustrates the active concern of Divine Love to a passerby who ultimately cannot resist the soul of Your Divine Countenance.

Dear Lord, like this Simon, allow me not to fear to have compassion for all those You have suffered for, especially the people who are part of my day-to-day existence. Simon, as You so well know, Lord, was at first reluctant because he was fearful. But looking into Your human eyes, Simon deeply recognized You as Lord.

Simon, through You, saw God in action! What action? That of God the Father sending Jesus His Son to the Cross. He saw Jesus freely and willingly taking upon Himself the weakness and brokenness of human existence. He saw Jesus in His humanity feel the crushing weight of the tree. Love followed respect; and Simon could only reach out with responsive love. And as he did that, he walked the privileged walk with You.

Station Six

VERONICA OFFERS HER
VEIL TO JESUS

Station Six of the Via Dolorosa stops the pilgrim just beyond an arched passageway bridging the buildings on either side. Here, tradition likes to remember an act of compassion shown to the Savior along His death walk. The arched door there now is said to stand on a significant site. Here was the house of a woman known in Christian folklore who probably never existed in reality.

Veronica, a follower of Christ, is said to have appeared on her doorstep with a clean linen cloth she had refreshed with water. When Jesus stopped here to turn toward her, she used the cloth to wipe His bleeding and dusty face. Apocryphal accounts identify her as the unnamed woman with a twelve-year history of hemorrhage whom Jesus had healed. When the veil came away from the face of Jesus, it is said, His image was printed upon it.

It is possible that in this account there is a variation on the later stories of the Shroud of Turin. Christians, even in the first centuries after Christ, had heard of the full-length image of the dead Savior miraculously imprinted on His burial cloth.

One version of Veronica's image of Jesus was preserved for some years in the Vatican in Rome. Then, close examination revealed it to be some sort of copy. The Shroud, on the other hand, has continued to prove itself to be a mysterious image of a crucified man living in the same place and time as Jesus of Nazareth.

In fact, there is no mention of any such woman or veil in any of the four Gospels. Veronica is probably a composite of those sympathetic Jewish women who undoubtedly lined the Way of the Cross in great numbers. Her name, authorities suspect, is a corruption of the Greek description of her transformed veil —*vera icone*—true image.

But this story was one which served well the Christian motive to dramatically recount the last journey of Jesus. In the late nineteenth century, the Greek Orthodox Church purchased the site of the traditional meeting of Veronica and Jesus. Preparing to erect another church there, they found the underground walls and arches of an older structure. This, they suspected, was part of the monastery of Ss. Cosmas and Damian, built in the sixth century for an order of nuns.

Some of the aged remains of the monastery, however, were sound enough to incorporate into the new church. St. Veronica Church, the result, was completed in 1895 but renovated by the Italian architect Antonio Barluzzi in the middle of the twentieth century. Here in this quarter of Jerusalem, the history of faith is literally layered, with one age on top of another.

Though the station which recalls the compassion of Veronica may not be found in one of those layers of true history, the marker surely evokes compassion and prayer among those who stop here. A fragment of a column built into the stone wall specifically witnesses to the station theme here. But there is little of real eye-catching interest for photographers who want to recapture the lesson here. That seldom stops those with cameras, however . . .

Just as Father DiOrio stands to one side of the massive door and just to the side of the station marker, a group of Christian pilgrims catches up to add their prayers. They ask him if they can take some photos of him before moving on. He agrees with a grin.

Smiling under the warm Jerusalem sun, these Christians following in the path of the Galilean have their own images fixed on film at Veronica's station. Images made in love, after all, are important.

HIS IMAGE OF GRATITUDE

"Angels of mercy" are forever to be found in precious moments of earthly pain. Theirs is the privilege to soothe; theirs is the power to calm and reassure, to offer solace, to lull the pain, the hurt, the wound of human heart and human flesh. Indeed, theirs is the privilege of Divine Providence to touch God in the visible tabernacle of His presence: in broken human lives.

An angel of mercy is God's external hand; it is God's nursing compassion for afflicted humanity. Shall we not hail in this sixth station of the cross the *compassionate nurse?*

According to tradition, there occurred an incident which is particularly touching both to our Lord Jesus, Who was being led forth to Calvary, and for us who need to reflect once again on the sensitivity of one offering compassion.

This incident, whether authentic or not, is certainly plausible at that moment when Jesus staggered on His painful death march. A woman stranger, not concerned about human respect, a woman both generous and brave, broke through the ranks and pressed forward right in front of the Prisoner. And with cloth in hand, with spirit of love, a heart of grief, she touched our Lord to wipe His battered and soiled face. It was to be a bandage never to be forgotten! The Prisoner gratefully accommodated her gesture. Anyone who serves God will not be forgotten. And so legend memorializes this brave angel of mercy with the immortal name of Veronica.

Only the virtue of compassion—that deep feeling of sharing the suffering of another—moved the noble lady in strength and with grateful soul (possibly sometime in the previous three years Jesus had done some kindness to her which she could never forget). Now was her precious moment, and a moment of encounter indeed! She gave Him her tender womanly mercy. Her suffering Savior accepted it.

With a fleeting glance she perceived all the tragedy of the hour at hand. As she intently watched this guiltless Prisoner at the point of total exhaustion, having trouble moving His bleeding feet, stumbling left and right, dizzy and unsteady as He tried to balance His own weight, she sympathetically absorbed His disfigured countenance and heard His cry for some kind of nursing. She offered Him her very own possession. She offered Him not only her spirit but her very own precious treasure: her veil. With it she gently, tenderly wiped His face. She caressed Him with an act of human kindness. Amid His pain, Jesus was soothed and comforted. This valiant woman's act was a loving sympathy.

Jesus took the towel, wiped His face with it and gratefully surrendered it back to her. *Healing is nothing more than each one of us sincerely forgetting ourselves and thrusting our lives unconditionally to Him Whom faith confirms as our Suffering Lord.* And this healing nurse, this tender caressing woman, lets flow from her heart a remembrance of Him.

Healing is two-sided. As the healed soul surrenders to God, He the healing Lord sends forth His own healing flame of gratitude; His healing flows forth as an act of gratitude from a wounded grateful God to a consoling creature. Jesus rewarded Veronica. Not only would he repay her with a name to be remembered as an inspiration, but this Suffering Redeemer permitted His sorrowful countenance to be depicted upon that veil-towel. When Veronica later unfolded it, can you imagine her intense astonishment!

Lord Jesus, You seek so ardently and continuously give the opportunity to imprint Your sacred presence upon us humans. How often You communicate sanctifying grace, infusing it in us by the miracle of opportunities for a new birth —a new chance! What can I say? There are no excuses to give. But I know what I can do. Yes, I will do it! Right now, unconditionally, without any reservations, I invite You into my heart. Come, Lord Jesus, come into my heart with Your holy presence. Jesus, my Lord, have mercy on me, on us, on all. Forgive!

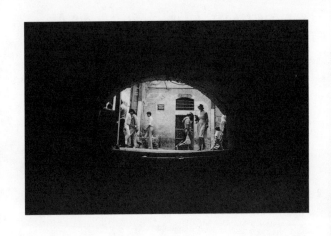

JESUS FALLS THE SECOND TIME

Following the Way of the Cross now takes Father DiOrio to the intersection of the Street of Dolors with that called Suq Khan ez-Zeit. Here toward the end of the street, the incline continues to be steep. A few steps farther and the seventh station comes into view just where the Street of the Dolors comes to a dead end. The station is marked near the door that leads to a station chapel.

But it is also marked in a sad way. The eyes of Father DiOrio and others cannot fail to catch it. Just to the right and below, garbage litters the ground. Candy wrappers, fruit peelings, the remains of items bought somewhere up the street, lie next to the wall where believers would like to honor their Savior, if only for a moment.

The case could be made that this is hardly the place for a station of the cross. After all, here is a prayer place in the middle of a well-worn pedestrian path. And yet there is a sense to some solemnity here. What took place here two thousand years ago didn't move people to respect either . . .

At this place, Jesus fell for a second time.

This time, however, Jesus went down without the cross to weigh Him down. As he looked up through his blood-matted hair, He might have seen a copy of his death sentence hanging next to one of the western gates. On that day, there was still a city gate at this place. It was familiar to the Jews simply as the Old Gate. Because of this incident, however, Christians later renamed it the Gate of Judgment. In the rebuilding of the city following its destruction in A.D. 70 and again in A.D. 135, there was no gate here because the walls of the city were pushed out to enlarge it.

It's quite possible that Jesus fainted here. The physical punishment, especially the blood loss and the daylong lack of food, would have drained the strength of the strongest man.

Roman response to that was undoubtedly a kick or whip laid across the fallen Jesus. Sometimes, too, the Condemned had a rope tied around His waist to facilitate a "quicker justice." A heavy yank on a rope around Jesus would have also brought him back to painful consciousness. Golgotha wasn't far from this gate and the soldiers wanted Jesus on the cross as soon as it could be done. And so, Jesus rose from the stone-paved street that was just one more marvel of Roman rule in Jerusalem.

Preparing to leave the city through one of the western gates must have sent a shudder through His body. In leaving Jerusalem, He

was now leaving the city of the Temple, the
city His Father had given to His chosen people
as a shining citadel.

"Jerusalem!" one of the Psalms rejoices.
"Encircled by mountains as Yahweh encircles
his people now and for always" (Psalms 125:2).
Jesus knew the Psalms so well. And He knew
just when His people would sadly recall the
Psalmist's praise and wonder about the day
they led Him outside the city walls to slaughter.

Meditation

FALL NUMBER TWO

Why did Jesus fall, not only once, twice, even three times, but perhaps many times? The most obvious reason was the torture inflicted on His humanity. Jesus endured physical exhaustion.

There is a moral reason, too. Human sin produced a mortal blow to the vital moral union between God and man. God the Creator, Who had created man out of nothing and endowed him with all nobility in the kingdom of all earthly existence, *was infinitely insulted.* The Evil One deceived and seduced the minds and the wills of the first man and woman. Accepting the false promises of Satan, the first parents of the earthly universe surrendered to a "Paradise Lost"; in their pride and disobedience, and believing that their choice was apparently good, they introduced into their own lives sin and its destruction. Because of sin Jesus had to become the human victim of redemption. Sin stimulated the enemies of Jesus to sentence Him *to the condemnation, to the suffering passion, to the Cross, to the death.* Sin, sin, sin! Sin alone caused Jesus to march to Calvary in such scorn and humiliation.

And so, as for Jesus falling frequently, it is understandable once we consider the anguishing ordeals a condemned prisoner has to undergo prior to his crucifixion. And Jesus had been taken prisoner the night before. He was treated with even worse flogging than other criminals. Being such a victim of sport and sadistic torment, He is drained; He is consumed from the multiple moral and physical assaults. It is a wonder—a miracle of love—that He still could go on! But then, love drums up untapped inner resources!

And so, in connection with the second fall of our Blessed Lord under the weighty beam of the cross, we devotees cannot help but grasp not only the physical reason but also the ultimate causative factor of such holistic human anguish, namely, evil and the effects of sin, be they deadly separations from God or slight infractions impeding a closer walk with God.

All sin, deadly or venial, is a disobedience to the will of God. And so Jesus, to restore the moral order, chooses to experience the effects of His Father's displeasure, and so subjects Himself to *temporal punishment.*

Dear Jesus, my indiscretions, my imprudencies, my destructive acts toward both self and others, block my good desires to never repeat sin. Though I desire to be strong, my experiences indicate repetitive weaknesses. I sincerely feel grief for having caused You displeasure. How often my faults and my unruly, evil inclinations have waged continual rebellion against my good intentions.

Lord, I have committed so many infractions in my lifetime, so many faults and even sins! Oh how true this confession is! But I know what I shall do: *I shall become like David, a man closest to Your heart. Like him I shall repent. What I have neglected to do in the past, I now resolve to repair. Please, Lord, waken in my heart a strong lively goodwill for Christlike living.*

Have mercy, Lord, have mercy!

JESUS SPEAKS TO THE WOMEN OF JERUSALEM

The next stopping spot for the pilgrim on the Via Dolorosa is just a few steps from the seventh station. Crossing the street Suq Khan ez-Zeit, Father DiOrio lifts up the hem of his cassock and continues the climb into still another street with another difficult name, Aqabat el-Khanqa.

This station stone here is not large. It is set into the wall of the Greek Orthodox church and convent called St. Charalambos. Inside the church, however, an altar also commemorates the station. Outside, within the stone, a Latin cross is surrounded with the Greek acronym NIKA, which means "Conqueror." Jesus conquered sin through suffering and death, not peoples by subjugation. With Latin and Greek symbols, the stone presents a quiet symbol of what must have been a tearful exchange.

It was customary in Jerusalem for the women to prepare a special drink for the condemned. It contained wine mixed with some myrrh, a combination that acted to dull the senses and thus to reduce pain. But if the women offered the drink to Him here, He re-

fused it as He later did from His cross. Jesus
wanted to remain fully conscious during his
ordeal.

Other scholars believe that the eighth station represents just what the Gospel of Luke
saw in it—a last chance for Jesus and the
women who followed Him to express love and
concern for each other. According to Luke, the
women had been following the condemned
Christ and "mourned and lamented for him."

As always, Jesus was touched by true feelings, deep love. He turns to them with love but
then speaks really to a larger audience—to all
of Jerusalem. They are like the words He
spoke just a few days before. That was the day
He rode toward the city on a colt. The people
greeted Him with palms and shouts of greet-
ing. Like the message that day, this one
prophesies dark days for the city.

> Daughters of Jerusalem, do not weep
> for me; weep rather for yourselves and for
> your children. For the days will surely
> come when people will say, "Happy are
> those who are barren, the wombs that
> have never borne, the breasts that have
> never suckled!" Then they will begin to
> say to the mountains, "Fall on us!"; to the
> hill, "Cover us!"
>
> Luke 23:28–31

Jesus was talking of the decimation of the
city which was to occur about forty years later,

in A.D. 70. The Roman general Titus totally leveled the Holy City, including the Temple. As Jesus had predicted at Bethphage, before He rode into Jerusalem amid the hosannahs, not one stone was left on another in this city of stone when the Romans were done in A.D. 70.

From a spiritual perspective, the message of Jesus here undoubtedly focuses on far more than the future physical danger to the city. There is the theme of justice, of humanity's need for repentance. Such repentance would give life, He seems to say. Instead, as He can foresee, Jerusalem will choose death. It will not seek forgiveness for its life. Finally, however, life will be turned upside down anyway. In a culture where sterility was viewed as a curse, childlessness will be a blessing, motherhood a misfortune.

Of all the stations so far, Father DiOrio seems to be thinking, this is the saddest. Jesus falls, He endures the sad encounter with His mother, He must carry the cross. But all of that leads to triumph and Resurrection. This station, however, warns of disaster and the fruits of faithlessness. There will be no triumph for those who reject the way to life, Jesus predicts.

Now, Father DiOrio, just one priest on pilgrimage, turns to retrace his steps back down the Suq Khan ez-Zeit. Before he leaves, however, he reaches up to place his own small crucifix atop the Latin cross carved into stone. To teach repentance and the new life of healing here, as Jesus did—that too is the mission of this man on the Way of the Cross.

Meditation

A HEAP OF TEARS

Large numbers of people followed him, and
  of women too,
who mourned and lamented for him.

(Luke 23:27)

Consolation is a tender expression. And Jesus
was moved by those weeping women, the
daughters of Jerusalem, who in spite of their
own tears did not really know who He was.
Yet they believed Him innocent.

> Daughters of Jerusalem, do not weep
> for me; weep rather for yourselves and for
> your children. For the days will surely
> come when people will say "Happy are
> those who are barren, the wombs that
> have never borne, the breasts that have
> never suckled!"

Luke 23:28–29

Jesus saw their tears, and He heard their
cries. Jesus, a gentleman to the last, verbally
expressed His gratitude to these daughters of
Jerusalem. They had attempted to lessen His
grief, His sorrow, His disappointment. Jesus'
heart was moved by their solace and comfort.

After the robust Simon of Cyrene, who had

obeyed without a word and became himself sensitized by compassion for the Prisoner, lent his broad shoulders to relieve Jesus, some of the soldiers raised Jesus to His feet and urged Him onward. It was then that a few women, with heads customarily mantled in veils, followed in the wake of that Good Friday procession.

However, they were physically restrained by the military patrol and thus kept from close contact with Jesus the Prisoner. As echoes rising above and surging over the tumult, and mingled with all the other voices from the noisy mob, these women's cries and lamentations pierced the air. And as some of the patrol officers urged Jesus onward to Calvary, some of the faithful women (some perhaps whom Jesus must have blessed with a miracle in days past) suddenly pressed forward. They would not be kept at a distance any longer.

They knew that within a few moments they would no longer be able to touch Jesus, and so huddled together as a group they rushed toward Him. They were sobbing and weeping. They did not care about the curious onlookers or the accusers. *Love alone urged them!* Their sympathy and compassion shot straight to the heart of Jesus like an arrow hitting its mark. The enemies of Jesus from both the religious and the civic sides eyed them wrathfully.

For a moment Jesus was free from His burden of the cross: Simon was relieving Him of

His load. And so, Jesus, turning to these women, looked at them through blood-crusty, bloodstained and bloodshot eyes. Since His mouth was parched and His voice weakening, Jesus could only utter a few words: some gratitude, some comfort, some consolation. As Luke records, Jesus told them not to weep for Himself but to weep for themselves and for their children. The Lord had recognized their grief. It was their pledge and their love. He took the opportunity to strengthen these sympathetic human souls. He gave them their own needed consolation. His words were meant not as rebuke, but rather as strengthening guidance for those who suffer and who will suffer more still. With the omniscience of His Divine Person to Whom His human nature was in hypostatic union, He knew and He saw all the oncoming centuries' massacres and the ruins which would befall mankind—their children and descendants. He aroused their attention to true values: their own salvation and that of their relatives and friends.

Lord, as teacher and Master, as preacher of truth, You did not allow Your own personal sufferings to deter You from imparting values. In Your response to these courageous women You bestowed a great moment of grace. Their tears were not displeasing to You. They were most acceptable. Those tears were like tokens of sympa-

thy to Your afflicted sacred heart. Those words of Yours directed to these valiant women were also addressed to me. I need to shed sincere tears of repentance. Have mercy, Lord!

JESUS FALLS FOR THE THIRD TIME

Because the Greek convent of St. Charalambos really stands in the byway of the Via Dolorosa, the pilgrim must backtrack to a long flight of steps. The staircase is stone and Father DiOrio again goes up along this route to Calvary or Golgotha. The incline that pilgrims today ascend by stairs is the same that Jesus once covered without steps. He made His way up over rocks and brush. The rise itself was Golgotha, a rock mound that probably measured about sixteen feet high.

If Jesus had been weakened all along His Way of the Cross, it is clear that the effort of the climbing sapped His reserves even further. It is possible too that He walked the streets barefoot, though Scripture makes it clear that He had been given back His clothing after the scourging. Yet even half of the pressures and pains Jesus was carrying to the top of this hill would have justified another collapse.

Tradition suggests that it was here that the Redeemer fell for a third time. This plunge to the hard earth would have put more dirt on the face of the Galilean and possibly more bruises too. There was little strength left to shield His head and face from direct blows from the ground. If the Shroud of Turin is to be considered the actual burial cloth of Jesus, it gives testimony to injuries to the cheeks and nose which another fall could help to explain.

The upright portion of the cross on which Jesus would die was already sunk into the summit of Golgotha, most authorities agree. Jewish law forbade execution within the city walls. Some years earlier the Romans had observed that prohibition by making this hillock their site of execution. It was outside the city. But it was also close enough to be seen by hundreds of Jews traveling to and from Jerusalem. That fulfilled Rome's goal—to make an example of anyone who challenged the empire's authority. Sometimes, the crucified were left on the crosses for days . . .

By this point, Father DiOrio himself has come to the top of the twenty-eight steps. This is the top of the hill known by the Latin Calvary or the Aramaic Golgotha. Both words conveyed the idea of a skull. There are other Christian pilgrims nearby now. Some of them recognize the minister of healing from the United States but there is a quiet respect for this journey. Each is making his or her own journey up this Via Dolorosa.

Near the entrance of St. Anthony's, the Coptic church here, the ninth station marker is found. It is again a simple station. A shaft of an ancient column is enclosed in a pillar near the door. It is almost inaccessible and easy to overlook. The stone walls of St. Anthony's rise on either side of the pillar, forming a kind of corner for a pilgrim's quick prayer. Father DiOrio kneels on the step and touches the station pillar.

Beneath the foundations of St. Anthony's, a cistern was found. Tradition suggests that the cross of Jesus was thrown into the cistern after he was taken down from it. A door just to the left of the spot where Father DiOrio still kneels leads to another church. It is called the Church of St. Helena, the mother of Constantine. She is credited with the finding of the cross.

FALL NUMBER 3

Perseverance is symbolic of determined purpose. It is stimulating. It harbors within itself perspective, purity, power! It becomes its own dynamo, a device for human power and action. It enables one bravely to weather life's turbulent storms. It is as persistent in its course as it is constant in its purpose. It charges one forward in task, regardless of obstacles and in spite of discouragement, for within it resides conviction and belief. It means not giving up!

In this our prayerful journey with Jesus to Calvary we have already meditated on two of Jesus' falls. Now we see our dear Lord drop to the ground a third time. The centurion had begun to worry about the Prisoner Jesus since he knew that Jesus had been scourged, and was therefore right at the brink of utter exhaustion. He witnessed Jesus trying awfully hard to hold Himself erect. The pounds of the fresh-cut timber, still green within its fibres, which Jesus was bearing, was extremely weighty. Jesus staggered frequently. His eyes were blurry. He could scarcely focus them on the backs of those rough soldiers who were leading Him on this forced march.

The distance to Golgotha measured approximately a thousand paces (three thousand feet), winding through narrow roads that we today would probably call alleys or passageways. Their width was approximately twelve to fifteen feet. Houses and shops dotted the paths, attached to one another.

Jesus could not move any faster. His steps kept faltering; He was swaying from side to side with the heavy tree wood across His scapular area. He was soiled, dirty, muddy and bloody. And as He staggered forward, the crowd of "rubberneckers" were scrutinizing Him. Some of the people showed pity; others were just downright indifferent. Others, through whispering tones or audible shouts, were most probably gratifying their sadistic impulses. They encouraged the soldiers to hurry with the dirty business of nailing the prisoner. It was a day of little sympathy and much hatred.

Jesus tried physically to persevere. Morally He was dauntless. He would go to Calvary; He would honor His Father. He would obtain and offer salvation—a New Birth to whoever would want to repent and receive Him as Savior and Lord. And so Jesus tried to go on: one foot at a time, one foot in front of the other. But His human body could not drag the other foot forward. He tried, and He tried. But He just could *not*. The huge weight of tree on His shoulders swayed. Jesus' entire body lost balance; He went out of physical control. He became dizzy. And Jesus fell.

The crowds heard the wood thump heavily on the white cobblestones. Jesus landed on His knees. His wounds cracked open again and He bled anew—fresh rivulets of blood from the thorns, the extremities, the lacerations all over His body. Everything seemed so useless!

Dear Jesus, redemption, reconciliation, regeneration and righteousness do not come cheaply. The heavy price is You! It will always be You! The blood which Your enemies craved was dripping, falling, draining itself from Your human vessel of flesh. As that special city of Jerusalem cast You outside of its walls, Your bloodstains could not be erased nor scrubbed away from its very stones. Death by Your haters is fast approaching. Even Nature shared the mood of a dying Man: the earth quaked as if in regurgitation, a reaction of repulsion over the fact that man could hate God!

O dear Lord, You are so holy. Your gifts of peace and righteousness are for everyone. Lord, they can be possessed by anyone who desires and wills to persevere to the end in Your grace. The person who refuses will need to blame only himself or herself. Intercede patiently for us, dear Lord, that we will accept Your invitation to become freshly created with a new heart, a clean heart, a grateful heart, a heart always valuing the gift of gift-giving, the Gift of Yourself!

JESUS IS STRIPPED OF HIS GARMENTS

All of the remaining stations of the cross are now clustered near to Calvary. In our day, it is difficult to visualize what the scene must have been originally like. Calvary, the tomb and the last five stations are all sites once visited in the open air and under the scorching sun of Palestine. Now, they are enclosed by the great Christian monument the Basilica of the Holy Sepulcher.

As a whole, the remaining stations, so close together, symbolize the reality that the earthly journey of Jesus was drawing to a close here. He had few steps to go, little time to live. The last dramatic events were happening very close together, as though a film were suddenly being shown at a faster speed.

In fact, however, everything was happening at the pace His Father had in mind. Perhaps it is just for pilgrims that His end was coming much too fast. Those following Jesus on His Way of the Cross also have few steps to make now.

Here, Father DiOrio stops for the tenth time to remember the stripping of Jesus as a prelude to crucifixion. Little can be said to Christians about this added suffering of Jesus. The sentence of crucifixion was intended to demean the victim in every way possible. The Church of the Holy Sepulcher marks this event in an austere fashion near the place which today is built over Calvary. Each of the Gospels alludes to this act as one of the final assaults on Jesus as a person.

Crucifying the condemned was compulsory for the four Roman soldiers who were with the Galilean on that spring afternoon on Golgotha. But it was obviously not a pleasant duty. Roman superiors therefore permitted legionnaires to divide whatever spoils the condemned had. The next of kin or friends had no claim on them.

In the case of Jesus of Nazareth, these worldly holdings amounted to little. It's likely that the sum total included only sandals, a head scarf, an undershirt, a cincture, an outer garment or mantle and a tunic which covered the body from neck to ankles.

As the evangelist John points out, the soldiers had divided most of the clothing Jesus had soon after He was on the cross. His tunic, they found, however, was woven all of one piece. This made it more valuable than the rest of the garments together. A woven garment divided four ways was worthless.

Under the eyes of Jesus, the soldiers finally decided to cast lots or dice for ownership of the tunic. The Man Whose last possessions they were taking was watching. Words from one of the psalms must have come to Him—"they divide my garments among them and cast lots for my clothes" (Psalms 22:18). From the cross, Jesus was fully aware that all of the prophecies concerning Him were being fulfilled minute by minute. And so, soon, Jesus was ready to leave the world in total poverty, much as He had entered it.

STRIPPED FOR SACRIFICE

And they stripped Him . . .

When the soldiers had finished crucifying
   Jesus
they took his clothing and divided it
into four shares, one for each soldier. . . .
                    John 19:23

The procession reached the Place of the
Skull: it was the hill called Calvary on
Golgotha's slopes. The anguishing walk had
been for Jesus a very long, difficult and laden
one. This poor Jesus, the Nazarene from Galilee, began to see through His befogged eyes the
spot on Calvary's heights where He would
complete the human sacrifice of His life.

Some of us who were privileged to visit Jerusalem still can see the Gennath Gate. When
the commanding centurion arrived at that
gate, he nailed the daily notice of the pending
executions; on this particular day the name of
the Victim Prisoner was Jesus of Nazareth.
The notice also briefly stated the crimes de-
manding such a death penalty for the accused
and condemned.

Before arriving, Jesus must have seen the

spot where His earthly purpose would be fulfilled. His physical eyes captured a distant image and magnified it, just as a camera's zoom
lens brings a far-off object into focus. There it
was: that hill of rock, stone and dirt, heaped
with garbage. There Jesus would die that you
and I could live. Just a few more paces would
definitely bring Him to that pinnacle!

Now the climb up that rounded, chalky
knoll whose shape resembles a skull. It is a
spot where the roads to Jaffa and Damascus
intersect. We who were there on pilgrimage in
August of 1984 can still remember this area; so
many passing pilgrims, commercial enterprises, traders, and so much hustle and bustle!
Upon that knoll this Jesus of Nazareth certainly would be seen by all. His excruciating
execution would be an "example" to all those
who witnessed it.

Everything was happening so fast! When the
awful moment for crucifixion had arrived, the
fury of that irrational mob struck Jesus, Who
was as gentle as a lamb. An added humiliation
for Jesus was nudity. His tormentors immediately stripped Him of His clothing violently.
Jesus felt this affliction both as a bitter bodily
pain and, even more, as a bitter violation of
His pure soul.

All the wounds which Jesus had received in
the scourging were now once again torn open.
His garments, saturated with His flowing
blood, now adhered to His mangled flesh.

Whole pieces of flesh and of skin were torn away, ripped open, as the executioners pulled Jesus' woolen homespun garments. The wounded Jesus sensed the humiliation of exposure to both the human observers and the elements of nature. His body received the cool air, caressing His inflamed, burning, feverish flesh. And as they stripped Him, the sights of the hill upon which He was standing brought rapid images to His mind. Calvary, as He could see from the debris around Him, was a garbage heap. That meant hundreds of insects and flies meandering and buzzing away, insects to feast on Jesus' wounded and bloody flesh.

Lord, what sort of love is this: such pain, such humiliation, such anguish and inhuman torture? It can only be called the love of the Divine!

Have mercy, O Lord, have mercy!

JESUS IS NAILED TO HIS CROSS

Up a flight of fourteen steps in the basilica, the wayfarer on this Via Dolorosa comes to the top of the hill called Calvary or Golgotha. The basilica, built over the hill, is divided here into two naves, one devoted to the Roman rite, the other to the Greek Orthodox. And so in a few moments, Father DiOrio arrives at the Roman nave on the right. There is a sixteenth-century silver-plated bronze altar from Florence, Italy. This altar and a mosaic above it represent the focus of the eleventh station, the crucifixion.

The altar, designed by a Dominican priest, depicts six scenes of the Passion. Father Dominic, O.P., designed the whole for the Stone of the Anointing which today is displayed near the central basilica entrance on the floor below.

A massive twentieth-century mosaic above the altar also illustrates the eleventh station here. Jesus, arms and legs outstretched on a fully assembled cross, lies waiting to be raised with it to the top of the hill. A grieving Mary stands above Him looking at her Son while a soldier with extra nails in one hand, a hammer in the other, oversees his work.

Father DiOrio kneels to honor the message that this station brings to Christians—that Jesus endured almost indescribable punishment in order to redeem all men.

Authorities believe that when Jesus was pulled down to the ground to be nailed He was stretched out against the crossbeam. When the nails were driven into the wrists (not through the palms of the hands as is typically represented), then Jesus was helped to stand nailed to the crossbeam. Probably three or more soldiers hauled the crossbeam and Jesus with ropes to the top of the upright and secured it there with a hook or dropped it into a pre-carved niche.

Ancient sources report that there was, in addition, a thin wooden wedge at the front of the cross which the crucified straddled. Its function was to support the weight but it also prolonged the dying and hence the suffering of the condemned. After Jesus was positioned on the now assembled cross, a nail or nails were driven through the feet, which were crossed one over the other.

When the body of Jesus was secured to the cross, the soldiers hammered a placard above His head which read, "Jesus of Nazareth, the King of the Jews." Pilate had ordered them to do so. It was usual for the crucified to merely wear the charge for which he was dying around his neck during the public walk to the site of crucifixion.

This one was inscribed in Hebrew, Latin, and Greek, thus ensuring that virtually everyone who saw it would be able to read it. Pilate apparently knew that the public display of a sign, "King of the Jews," would irritate the Jewish leadership. Masses of people would be coming and going through the Ephraim Gate near Golgotha. The Jews immediately appealed to Pilate to have it removed. But the procurator refused, preferring to see them endure some ridicule about "their king."

From the Gospel of St. John, the eyewitness among the evangelists, it seems clear too that the cross raised Jesus considerably above the ground. Possibly, He could even see over the city wall to the tops of buildings He knew well. But it is obvious that He would have watched for a while as large crowds gathered to witness His execution.

NAILS FOR A KING

This is Calvary. This is the moment of moments! Its mystery of love has arrived! Jesus is being hauled into the air, nailed to a tree, between heaven and earth! This is the moment of the Apostolate of Redemption. And the Redeemer is doing His work perfectly!

As we pass Him fettered on a tree, we the observers can only see how history is in its making and how history is in its balance: namely, the sin of man, the love of God.

The human countenance of Jesus was being disclosed to any passerby who happened to look beyond His tattered flesh. There hung the Divine and Holy Savior, squirming like a worm, alternately chilly and sweaty—consumed with fever! The blows of the picks, only a few minutes before, could still be heard in the memory of Jesus as the soldiers dug holes into the rocky ground which would soon receive and support the crosses of Jesus and the two thieves also condemned to die with Him—one on either side.

The centurion in charge finally gave the order for crucifixion. Jesus was the first! The executioners very gruffly and quickly thrust our

Lord upon that awful bed of wood. Jesus could see the hammer raised high to hit the nails. Flesh and bone were pierced, blood squirted out. This is what sin has done to Him who would give life and love to those that would offer nothing more than hateful death. Jesus had promised to suffer all these things, even unto the end.

Calvary was and is very personal: an interaction by which sentiments must be shared between sinner and saint, between sinful man and redeeming God. This act of crucifixion was no game. Through His Passion and death, through the victory of the Resurrection, Our Lord was exercising His divine mission to all: the apostolate of *reconciliation.*

> And since when we were His enemies, we were brought back to God by the death of His Son, what blessings He must have for us now that we are His friends, and He is living within us!
>
> Romans 5:10 *(Living Bible)*

> The love of Christ impels us who have reached the conviction that since one died for all, all died. He died for all so that those who live might live no longer for themselves, but for Him who for their sakes died and was raised up.
>
> 2 Corinthians 5:14–15 *(NAB)*

But now Christ has achieved reconciliation for you in his mortal body by dying,
so as to present you to God holy, free of
reproach and blame.

Colossians 1:22 *(NAB)*

My dear reader and partner in prayer, I
have taken you, as I have taken myself so
often, to Calvary's mystery. Twice, so far, God
has granted me the privilege through my
friend, Sir John Hodgson, of the Catholic
Travel Agency of Chevy Chase, Maryland, of
celebrating Holy Mass on the very spot of this
deicide: the crucifixion site. You and I, through
prayer and meditation, have now arrived at a
point where it would be best for soul to speak
to soul.

The center of Christianity is a personal relationship with Jesus. It is a matter of experience; and we each are summoned to experience
Jesus as Savior. This involves not knowing
about Him but *knowing Him* as a person. The
best way to experience His love for you and for
me is to experience that salvific moment of His
crucifixion through prayer, meditation and
compassion.

Dear Lord, this act of crucifixion was no game.
The cross and the nails were not toys. The ham-
mer is definitely steady and certainly direct. Its
repetitive downward blows are penetrating. This
is no game, Dear Lord. The stakes were high:
my soul in balance, your life in balance. The
result: lost or saved, heaven or hell!

JESUS DIES ON THE CROSS

It is just a few steps to the left into the Greek nave of Calvary and to the twelfth station. Father DiOrio moves to this station, where Jesus died on the cross. He kneels to honor the memory of the spot as every believer must. In this place, verified as the crucifixion site, Jesus Christ redeemed mankind.

The Greek Orthodox remembrance of the event is a central altar supported by columns. But beneath that altar is a smaller altar which displays a metal disk toward the middle. In the center of this disk, made of precious materials, is a round opening. Beneath the opening a hole is burrowed into rock, the rock of Golgotha. In this hole, it is believed, the cross of Jesus was anchored and here was supported the dying, crucified body of Jesus of Nazareth.

From the time he was crucified, about noon, till the time of his death, about 3 P.M., Jesus suffered terrifying agonies.

Crucifixion meant losing blood drop by drop. There was also additional loss of body fluids, however. Through sweating and because he had not had anything to drink, Jesus began to suffer terrible thirst and dehydration.

His mouth, nose and throat began to feel parched.

The pain from the nail wounds into the wrists would have been the most excruciating. That's because the nails were likely to have pierced the median nerves. To relieve the pressure on those wounds, the crucified typically tried to lift the weight or drag off the wrists by raising himself upward from the wooden wedge or seat beneath him.

As the hours went by, however, more and more muscles constricted and any added movement of the victim became more and more painful. Even chest muscles became constricted, making it increasingly difficult to breathe. Toward the end, Jesus began to struggle for breath.

According to all four evangelists, the Savior spoke seven times from His cross in the three hours of His dying. He asked His Father to forgive those who crucified Him. He promised paradise to the good thief. He asked His disciple John to care for His mother Mary. Much closer to His death, He spoke four times. He cried out to God asking why He had been forsaken. Then He complained of thirst. After receiving the wine-soaked sponge on the spear tip, He said that His work was accomplished. Lastly, He said he was commending His spirit into His Father's hands.

Three of the last seven statements Jesus made, scholars point out, directly touched on or fulfilled messianic prophecies written so many centuries before Him. The cry about abandonment is directly quoted from the first line of Psalm 21. The appeal for relief from His thirst paraphrases the laments in two later psalms about the suffering Savior. His statement, "It is accomplished," reported by John alone, referred to His fulfillment of all the prophecies made about Him and the fulfillment of His mission.

At that point, St. John, who was there, said that Jesus first bowed His head and "then gave up his spirit." He did not die first with His head then falling onto His chest.

From the sixth to the ninth hours, the dying hours of Jesus, darkness had covered the land. The claim by the evangelists has been confirmed by contemporary historians. Whether it was a dust storm building up over Jerusalem or a divine intervention in the heavens (or both) is not known. At the moment of the death of Jesus, an earthquake occurred and the veil in the Temple was torn in two from top to bottom. The rock tombs of many in the Jerusalem area were broken open.

At just about the exact moment Jesus was bowing His head to die, lambs were being led into the Temple for slaughter. These were the innocent lambs without blemish for the Passover meals. To fulfill Jewish rituals, the blood of each lamb had to be entirely drained from the body. A few minutes after His death, the body of Jesus was pierced with a Roman lance. Blood and then water drained out, indicating that all of the blood of His body had been given up much like that of a Passover lamb.

Though not even the followers of Jesus realized it, the death of Jesus gave birth to a new kind of Passover for God's people. But in the hearts of those just rising off their knees, looking up at the dead Jesus, there was at this moment only grief.

THE SON OF GOD HAS BEEN SACRIFICED

And so it came to pass that the Son of God had been crucified. Love had turned sour, like wine that is left exposed. Evil entered the enemies of Jesus and spewed out its venom. Man, lofty and rational created being, reverted to the behavior of the animal, almost as hounds gluttonous for flesh and blood.

The cross was to be raised to an upright position. The executioners were hastening about in some confusion. Then the officer in charge gave them the command. They set to work. The stronger ones endeavored to lift the cross from the ground; others pulled on ropes, some steadied the cross as they directed it into the shoveled and picked holes. With a thunderlike sound, the cross dropped into its hole. The body of Jesus, its own weight compounded by the gravity of the dropping cross itself, shook. More ripping pain to His pierced hands and feet! More lacerations in His sinews and flesh!

The rough executioners tried to steady the heavy cross. They shook and turned right and left, to and fro the wooden beams bearing the hanging frame of their crucified victim. They fixed it finally and steadied it into restful position. The finishing touch was added as they fastened the cross in its place. They bound and hammered great blocks of wooden pegs, wedging them securely around the base. There Jesus hung like a wounded bird pinned through hands and feet.

The story of the shed blood never ends! His shed blood keeps shedding copiously, flowing out like rich red rivers. It was Redemptive Shed Blood! The ground soaked up its gushing torrents like a sponge. It seemed more welcoming to redemption than those humans who needed redemption most.

The Mother of Sorrows was standing there. St. John was near to her, very near indeed. He held her tenderly. The Mother of Sorrows turned pale with horror. St. John held her more tightly. The friends of Jesus were petrified. Frozen in terror and grief. They listened to His last words of forgiveness. His pain was now finished!

Lord Crucified, words which are so easily and cheaply spoken are at this moment unspoken. This horrendous evil deed has stunned us. I want to speak to you, Lord. As I walk by Your cross, my heart must break forth. Ah, I know what I shall pray . . .

I slipped His fingers
I escaped His feet

I ran and hid
For Him I feared to meet.

One day I passed Him
Fettered on a tree
He turned His head and
Looked and beckoned me.

Neither by speech nor strength
Could He prevail
Each hand and foot was
Pinioned by a nail.

He could not run nor
Clasp me if He tried
But *with His eyes*
He bade me reach His side.

For pity's sake, thought I,
I'll set you free
Nay—take this cross, said He
and follow me.

This yoke is easy
This burden light
Not hard nor grievous
If you wear it tight.

And so did I follow Him
Who could not move
An *uncaught* captive
In the hands of love.

JESUS IS TAKEN DOWN FROM THE CROSS

There is, of course, deep grief in Christians who rise from the scene of the crucifixion even today. But there is a greater joy. With that sort of mix in his heart, Father DiOrio gets up from the crucifixion site and moves a step or two to the right.

Here stands the Latin altar which marks the removal of the body of Jesus from His cross. Instead of a view of the corpse of Christ, the scene is a statue of the "Stabat Mater," the "Pierced Mother," Mary. As the prophecy of Simeon had foretold so many years before, a "sword" of deep grief did pierce the heart of the Mother of Christ.

Statues represent the Latin-rite expression throughout the basilica while icons, frequently overlaid with silver or gold, represent the Greek style. This statue brings to the altar some of the best work of sixteenth- or seventeenth century Portugal. It was sent to the Holy Land in the late eighteenth century. Covered with precious jewels and gold, it represents the offerings of princes and peasants of that age.

It is hard to say for certain that the Mother of Jesus was present when the body of her Son was taken down from the cross. Possibly, the apostle John took her into his care immediately and spared her the added horror of that scene. The Pietà artists of a hundred generations would have us believe otherwise, however. And it is, of course, possible that she, as his only living relative, stayed to see that the body of Jesus was properly cared for.

Joseph of Arimathea, according to all four Gospels, went immediately to Pilate to ask for permission to take down and bury Jesus. He owned an unused rock tomb about twenty-five yards from the crucifixion site. The body of Jesus would be laid there. Assured finally that the Nazarean had indeed died so quickly, Pilate agreed to the request. In general, it was Roman practice to leave the bodies of the crucified on the cross for some time after death as a warning. But it was Jewish practice to bury the dead before sundown. Passover made that even more crucial.

St. John says that Joseph's charitable efforts were then joined with those of Nicodemus, a Pharisee who, like Joseph, had become a follower of Jesus.

By the time the two were able to begin to bring the body of Jesus down from His cross, it could have been after 4 P.M. It is likely that both men, as wealthy leaders of the community, had male slaves to help them. They would have been needed. Some heavy work was involved.

First of all, the nails through the feet of Jesus would have been removed. Then, the crossbeam with the body of Jesus still fixed to it would have been lifted up off the upright and slowly lowered down in pulley fashion with ropes. If the Shroud of Turin is indeed the burial cloth of Jesus Christ, authorities estimate that Jesus was a well-built man. Taller than average for the era, he was about five feet, eleven inches tall and weighed about 170 to 175 pounds.

Was there time then to wash the body as Jewish custom required? It is not certain that there was. Shroud authorities suggest that the body of the man wrapped in that cloth had not been washed. Too many clotted bloodstains were imprinted on the remarkable linen. A good cleansing of the body would have washed away these traces of tragedy.

In any case, with the sun dipping lower and lower into the sky and with Passover close at hand, the body of Jesus was placed in a linen burial shroud. Additional bindings were wrapped around His head and hands. The women who loved and followed Jesus watched to see the tomb where He was being laid. They planned to return on the day after the Sabbath to complete the burial rites and customs.

A MOTHER KEPT HER VIGIL

In general, the word "courage" conjures up in the mind heroic acts of soldiers, sailors, knights of the past centuries, men of valor, characters of daring enterprises—all, however, excluding women. Even Shakespeare is read as having placed upon the lips of Hamlet: "Frailty, thy name is woman!"

How untrue such a statement, let alone such a thought! God made a woman to be the mother of His Son. This woman, from the first dawn of Christianity, represents the antithesis of frailty. She is the Woman who became the Victorious Lady of Courage, a Mother who stood beneath the cross and thus became the Mother of you and me at the cost of pain and grief, of bitter suffering; and all because she bore faith.

A mother is unique in both her being and in her spirit. St. John, from his firsthand observation on Calvary's heights during that horrendous moment, wrote:

Near the cross of Jesus stood his mother . . .

John 19:25

Mary was not a spectator. She was there as a courageous mother! That entire awful day might have been like a bad dream. But it was not. She saw them give her Son a crossbeam for crucifixion. She watched the centurion proudly riding his horse. She saw it all; every bit she saw! The crowds, the jeering laughter, the scorn and the spittle hurled at her Son. She heard the foul language, the biting sarcasm. As she walked the same road she looked down at the blood drops, sinking dryly into the sands and upon the cobbles. She saw the crosses, the thieves forced to be companions to her Son. Mary saw Him bend under the weight of the cross. She saw Him vacillate and fall three times. She gazed at the brutes who surrounded Him, kicked Him, ordered Him to get up with their beatings and cursing. She tried often to run to Him as He continued His climb, but she was held back by both the soldiers and the onrushing crowd.

Finally, Calvary came, and she consumed the bitter chalice to its last drop. There, upon that platform, Mary witnessed Him harshly stripped of His garments that were stuck to His bleeding wounds. She observed the lacerations—all of them! And to make her sorrow more agonizing, the sound of the clanging hammer nailing Him, hand and feet, reverberated painfully in her ears, blow by wrenching blow.

Let us stand with her as she sees Him ele-

vated and plunged into the ground with arms
outstretched, forming the first crucifix. She
looks at her Son pinned there on that awful
cross. He looks like a common criminal. His
head occasionally bobbing, His chin touching
His chest at times. His entire weight sus-
pended, His knees bent forward. The executioners perform the ritual with religious accu-
racy. They nail the right foot over the left, and
feet are pulled downward, nailed very closely
together at the base of the cross. Life, it would
seem to His executioners, is cheap. Mary hears
every sigh, cry, groan. She hears every word
that erupts from her tortured Son: "Father,
forgive them . . . This day you will be with
Me in paradise . . . I am thirsty . . . My
God, my God, why have You deserted me?
. . . Into Your hands I commend My spirit
. . . It is finished!" And those unforgettable
words: "Woman, this is your son; John, this is
your mother!"

With every word, with every movement of
her dying Son, Mary experiences profound sorrow. But she has sublime courage! Motherly
heroism! All that she could do was simply
stand there and give her Son her presence. She
stood there with the virtue of silence. Mary did
not go away from the cross. "In silence and in
hope shall Your strength be" (Isaiah 30:15).

How remarkable in suffering is the nobility
of this woman. Mary did not once utter a sin-
gle word against man's cruelty and injustice

toward her Son. No sign of impatience, no annoyance. She does not retaliate with imprecations. She does not call down the wrath of God upon her Son's enemies. She stands there, awash in tears. Like a mother who has been bruised or hurt, all she can do to strengthen her Son is to stay close by, near His hurt.

Mother of God, holy and dear Mary, I come before you to pray. As you stood by Jesus to console Him, may I stay near to you offering you my compassion and my filial love. O Mary, last August, and last April during Holy Week, I had the privilege of celebrating Holy Mass at this thirteenth station. I somehow felt your pain when Jesus was taken down from the cross and placed upon your knee, embraced by your arms, caressed anew with your maternal strokes. With you I feel the pain of that moment when you looked down upon His face and body. "Jesus is dead," you must have whispered. He speaks no more. His voice is stilled. His senses no longer function. They are broken and silenced in death.

Dear Mary, what can I do? The earthly-minded may never have time to comprehend your sufferings! How can I console you in your afflictions? O but yes, I do know how I can ease your pain. Yes, I can offer Jesus, your Son, that which He lived and died for: my soul . . . my soul . . . my immortal soul!

Dear Mary, be my mother. It is not a good

exchange. But Jesus wanted it that way. So please come to me. Accept me! Leave me not for an instant. The day of death will definitely come to me, ushering me into eternity. At that moment, especially, be at my side.

JESUS IS PLACED IN
THE TOMB

Father Ralph DiOrio rises now to follow Jesus
to the last station of the cross. The site, of
course, is the tomb of Jesus, which Christians
have marked since that day of sorrows almost
two thousand years ago. The authenticity of
the site has never been successfully challenged.

In the plan of this basilica, the pilgrim de-
scends the stairs again to the entry level of the
great church. Over toward the great doors,
past the Stone of the Anointing and into the
main basilica beneath the gigantic dome, pilgrims are directed.

The followers of Jesus, on the other hand,
carried His body down this same hill to an un-
known place where His body was wrapped in
cloth and sprinkled with spices. Then it was
carried a little farther and placed inside the
garden tomb of Joseph of Arimathea. This was
but a short way from the crucifixion site just
outside the city walls.

There beneath the dome, Father DiOrio now
sees the chapel which encloses the tomb. Some
chapel has protected the sacred spot since the
emperor Constantine reclaimed the tomb from

earth in the fourth century. This chapel is ornate.

Every generation and every Christian group has understandably wished to beautify the "place where they laid Him." A marble façade and pillars adorn the front. Lamps of precious metals and candlesticks given by every Christian denomination are to be found. The heavy scents of candle wax and incense fill the air.

But through the doorway, Christians can enter the small antechamber of the tomb. This today is called the Chapel of the Angel. Farther in, Father DiOrio now bows low to enter a small chamber in which the body of Jesus rested till Resurrection. This is the Tomb itself, a room which measures about six feet square. Dropping to his knees, he is soon lost in prayer to the God Who endured such suffering and death to be finally left dead in this place. Beneath is the actual stone shelf on which Jesus was laid. It runs the length of the chamber.

The tomb of Jesus was typical of its era, historians report. Burial in Jerusalem, a city so well endowed with stone quarries, meant burial in chambers or small rooms hollowed out of rock rather than burial in the ground. This tomb of Jesus was surrounded by a small garden, according to the Gospels. A stone much like a millstone had been pushed up a small rise and then wedged in place temporarily by a rock cut just for that purpose. Without doubt, the Gospels assure us, that task required a number of strong men, most likely the servants of Joseph and Nicodemus.

A stone ledge like the one on which Jesus was then placed was a standard feature of the burial chamber of this era. As a rule, the family or friends of the deceased returned to the tomb much later to collect the bones of the deceased from the stone shelf. These were then put in a sort of urn or ossuary elsewhere in the tomb or in a cemetery. This made the burial chamber available for the burial of others.

When the loved ones of Jesus had finished positioning the body and paying their last respects to Him, they went out to the stone "door" once more. Moving the wedge that had locked the huge wheel of rock in place, they watched now as it quickly rolled back into the carved recess. Now it was securely positioned in front of the entrance to the tomb. There was no way for one man to get out or for another to get in. Entering would again require considerable manpower.

Throwing a last sad look over their shoulders to the burial place of Jesus and to Golgotha, Joseph, Nicodemus and the others hurried now toward the city before the holy quiet of the Great Sabbath began. Through the Ephraim Gate they went, leaving Jesus of Nazareth in the tomb and in the hands of His Father.

ENTOMBED—BUT NOT FOR LONG

Not all those at Calvary's hill were enemies of Jesus. Many were there as helpless friends. Like Mary and St. John, and the woman at His feet, Mary of Magdala, all they could do was to stand by and to allow evil to take its course. But in the end, they could help by some act of courtesy, some sort of caring, in order to rectify; perhaps they could even minutely smooth out the tragedy of Jesus' death.

During His three-year apostolate of preaching and teaching and healing, Jesus found a friend who remained true to Him right up to the end. Yes, even beyond death: right to the very tomb! Jesus definitely had a friend in Joseph of Arimathea. This gentle old man was also rather wealthy. Among his possessions was a recently built personal tomb. It had been hewed out of rocks not too far away from Calvary's slope.

It was to this tomb that Joseph of Arimathea, accompanied by other friends of Jesus, with Mother Mary, St. John, Mary Magdalene and others, brought Jesus for burial.

St. John (19:39) states that Nicodemus had

purchased the appropriate mixtures of myrrh and aloes, about a hundred-pound weight. After the proper preparations were completed, they tenderly wrapped the corpse of the Lord in a clean cloth and shrouded it with cloths of fine linen. With utmost affection and reverence, the best expression of their human love, they entombed the Lord.

As they left, the entrance of the tomb was, as far as they could know, closed. They sealed it with the large rolling stone, approximately four or five feet in diameter.

The mystery of that grave, now Jesus' resting place, was that within that tomb the end was not at hand. Supernatural power, supernatural glory, was activating itself powerfully within the Holy Sepulcher. A lifeless body over which the laws of hate and death did their part was not to experience corruption or decay.

O Holy Sepulcher, what a glorious and venerable mystery lurks within you as Christ, Son of God, Savior of the world, rests—hides—within you!

Soon, very soon, the tomb would be empty. Soon, very soon, the Lord Jesus would appear; and He would confirm Who He was, and Why He came. Soon, very soon, men like Saul, an enemy of the Lord, would become disciples.

With the conviction that the tomb was empty, and with the added powerful religious experience of Jesus appearing to him, this Paul, this Saul of Tarsus—one of the first to receive a mighty anointing of the Holy Spirit—would himself go forth and teach the Ephesians, Thessalonians, Romans, Philippians. He would travel anywhere the Gospel of Christ urged him. He would be recorded as saying to the Corinthians:

> The chief message I handed on to you, as it was handed on to me, was that Christ, as the scriptures had foretold, died for sins; that He was buried, and then, as the scriptures had foretold, rose again on the third day. Then he was seen by Cephas, then by the eleven apostles, and afterwards by more than five hundred apostles, and afterwards by more than five hundred of the brethren at once, most of whom are alive at this day, though some have gone to their rest. Then He was seen by James, then by all the apostles; and last of all, I too saw Him, like the last child, that comes to birth unexpectedly.
>
> 1 Corinthians 15:3–8

THE RESURRECTION

In the practiced tradition of keeping the Way of the Cross, there is no fifteenth station. But in Christian belief, there is inevitably something to be said beyond the placement of Jesus in the tomb. The story clearly did not end there. And if it did, as St. Paul reminds believers of all times, it would merely be a sad story.

> If there is no resurrection of the dead, Christ himself cannot have been raised, and if Christ has not been raised then our preaching is useless and your believing it is useless; indeed, we are shown up as witnesses who have committed perjury before God, because we swore in evidence before God that he raised Christ to life. For if the dead are not raised, Christ has not been raised, and if Christ has not been raised, you are still in your sins. And what is more serious, all who have died in Christ have perished.
>
> 1 Corinthians 14:13–18

It is clear from each of the Gospels that the Resurrection of Jesus on the third day after His death on Calvary was His triumph over

Calvary. It also fulfilled the prophecies He had made about the sign of Jonah and the rebuilding of the Temple within three days and the less veiled prediction He had made about His resurrection.

It is just as clear from Scripture, however, that the followers of Jesus never really expected Him to rise from the dead. When He was taken from them in Gethsemane, they scattered. So too did their memories of what He had said of His suffering, death and resurrection.

After His death, according to St. Matthew, the high priests and elders had begun to worry over the predictions Jesus had made about His resurrection. If the body of Jesus was taken by His followers, they could claim that He rose from the dead and thus perpetuate His cult.

The Jewish leaders went to Pilate to ask that a guard be posted at the tomb. He released to their use the Roman soldiers assigned to the crucifixion detail. The Jews, however, made even further precautions. They took strips of cloth and stretched them tightly across the entrance of the tomb. On either end of the strips, they affixed wax seals right to the stone. It would be impossible for the body to be taken away, they reasoned, without telltale evidence of breaking open the seals. The guards and the seals were in place.

On the first morning after Sabbath, the women from Galilee who had followed behind

Jesus on His Via Dolorosa made their way to the garden tomb. When they were closer, they could see that the stone was now rolled away from the entrance. The Gospels vary, one from another, about what took place after that.

St. Matthew reports that the women had felt an earthquake on their way to the tomb. An angel appeared in front of the awestruck guards. Effortlessly, the angel then rolled away the stone that twenty men would have struggled under. The messenger of God then addressed the women, but these were words for all to hear, for the rest of time.

> There is no need for you to be afraid. I know you are looking for Jesus, who was crucified. He is not here, for he has risen, as he said he would. Come and see the place where he lay, then go quickly and tell his disciples, "He has risen from the dead and now he is going before you to Galilee; it is there you will see him." Now I have told you.
>
> Matthew 28:6–7

And so, the story began to be told.

In the dark, a new light was already finding its way into existence. The new light was Jesus of Nazareth. As in the freshest moments of Creation, something new was taking place. The martyred Son of God was rising from death. In the thinking of the Jews, this was the third day since His death.

Because Jesus had died before the Sabbath hours on the day of His death, it was as though it had happened the day before. In the reckoning of the Jews, a day began with sundown and ended with the sundown of the following day. The time after dusk was therefore seen as the second day after the death of Jesus even though He'd died just hours before. The third day was figured from that dusk of Holy Saturday. That was the day that had worried the Jewish leaders. History has proven their fears well founded.

On this late summer afternoon, Father Ralph A. DiOrio finishes this Way of the Cross and leaves the Basilica of the Resurrection here in Jerusalem. As few men can, this minister of healing has seen the Mystery of Redemption from the perspective of pain and from that of healing. It is clear how much in human agony that first Via Dolorosa cost Jesus. And yet as heavy as that cost was, there is, after all—as there will always be—Resurrection. Praise the Lord!

RESURRECTION PRAYER

My Lord God, You are the Christ Risen, and upon my heart You have written the rejoicing words of hope. *Calvary had no power to finish You. Calvary did not spare You. Your Resurrection released You! Dear Joseph of Arimathea along with some of Your closest friends gave You a tomb: Your body stopped there as its captive for two nights. And as You entered that tomb by these kind hands of Your friends You knew that You would very soon prove that* no tomb *could keep You captive because You are the power to rise again!*

My Lord Jesus, there can be no Christianity without Your Resurrection! You as fully immortal have risen, still, however, wanting to retain in Your hands and feet, in Your pierced side, the marks of humiliation, showing them as tokens in Your victorious exaltation.

My Resurrected Lord, "I Believe in the Resurrection of the Dead, and in the Life to Come!" Why do I believe this? Why am I so certain? Only because You, Lord Jesus, have given me authentic proof: You, Lord Jesus, appeared alive and well, glorious, victorious, to Your apostles, disciples and friends. And be-

cause of their experiencing You and their pro-claiming You as the Christ Risen, I am assured that story told is true: The tomb is empty!

Jesus, my Lord, my God, You did keep Your promise that once again clothed in human flesh You would breathe as God the presence of Your Holy Spirit, would walk again as man, would definitely break the portals of death by never allowing the tomb to be Your destiny, my destiny.

Lord and Savior, Resurrected Christ, Prince of Peace, King of Kings, thank You for leaving me Yourself not as a dead memory of One Who walked to the cross the condemned enemy of people, church and state, as One receiving His rightful due, but as One leaving me Your Living Presence!

HALLELUJAH!   HALLELUJAH!
    HALLELUJAH!